HOW TO SURVIVE A
MARRIAGE

Written & Illustrated by
Tom Carey

PRICE STERN SLOAN
Los Angeles

Front cover illustration by Rick Penn-Kraus

Copyright 1992 by Tom Carey
Published by Price Stern Sloan, Inc.
11150 Olympic Boulevard, Sixth Floor
Los Angeles, California 90064
Printed in the United States of America
10 9 8 7 6 5 4 3 2 1

Library of Congress Cataloging in Publication
Carey, Tom.
How to survive a marriage
by Tom Carey
ISBN 0-8431-3367-8
1. Marriage—Humor. I. Title
PN6231 . M3C36   1992
818' .5402—dc209   1-31436
                                   CIP

NOTICE: The information contained in this book is true and complete to the best of our knowledge. All recommendations are made without any guarantees on the part of the author or of Price Stern Sloan, Inc. The author and publisher disclaim all liability in connection with the use of this information.

This book has been printed on acid-free paper.

Dedicated

To my favorite married couples:
MikeandJudy
EricandTheresa
MaribethandJohn
PeggyandSteve
KathleenandPat
SusieandMick
MikeandJan
JimmyandJosie
TerryandKathy
ChuckandDebbie
And most of all to
MomandDad

About the Author

Tom Carey is a writer and illustrator who lives in Chicago.

His previous books include: *The Nun Book* (Turnbull & Willoughby, 1986), *The Modern Guide to Sexual Etiquette* (Turnbull & Willoughby, 1987), *Cliff's Notes Guide to Men* (Turnbull & Willoughby, 1988) and *Teed Off* (Taylor Publishing, 1991).

Table of Contents

Introduction:
What's Love Got to Do with It?

What is love? Perhaps it is like the rising sun ... aloof and distant, at first, creeping ever closer, ... silently, steadily ... until it envelops you in its great warmth and leaves you grouchy and sweaty, with those red lines across your back that you get from falling asleep on a lounge chair.

Perhaps love is like a muddy crocodile floating silently in a swamp, waiting, until you come blundering along, to snatch you up in its iron jaw and drag you thrashing and screaming to the murky depths.

The thing about happily ever after is, it only exists in fairy tales. And fairy tales always end after the big wedding day. That's because the Brothers Grimm were both married and knew the brutal realities of married life. If they didn't, they no doubt would have been known as the Brothers Giddy. How many books do you suppose the boys would have sold if they had ended their stories not with the famous phrase, " ... And they lived happily ever after," but with the more accurate, "And Prince Charming lounged around the castle in his boxer shorts for the rest of his days, swilling flagons of grog and watching ESPN highlights of last night's West Coast jousting matches"? And would generations of mothers have read their daughters bedtime stories about Cinderella and Sleeping Beauty, if it turned out that those two gals ended up as chubby, chain-smoking bingo addicts? I think not.

You may ask yourself, does marriage automatically render *every* relationship dull, boring, tedious, routine, tepid, lukewarm, uninteresting and sexless? Of course not! Some people have affairs. For that tiny percentage whose moral code won't abide such behavior (or for those who are afraid of getting caught), the statistics are less than encouraging. The problem is, it is darn near impossible to get reliable information about what married life is really going to be like once you tie the knot, or as the Maori tribe of the Galapagos says, once you "leap into the cauldron of eternal unpleasantness chained to your partner of peril."

Hell, your already-married friends are not going to share with you the whole truth about what goes on behind the closed doors of their little love nests. Not after they've spent the last couple of years billing and cooing in public, calling each other by truly icky nicknames and generally making everyone nauseous with their blather about how married life is just *super* swell and how damn *happy* they are. No, they're not about to give you even the tiniest little peek into their personal relationship HELL!

They won't tell you about the time she screamed her boss' name while in a passionate clinch with her beloved hubby. Nor will they tell you about how she discovered a shoe box full of perfumed love letters from his old girlfriend in the attic one day and decided to slice all his ties in half and unravel all his sweaters.

Certainly your parents are going to be of little help. They have a tough enough time remembering what happened *last week*, much less what happened during the first year they were married.

Of course, there are plenty of magazines filled with marriage "self-help" articles you can read. You know the ones— "WHAT 10 HOLLYWOOD STARS SAY WOMEN WANT IN A HUSBAND!" or "SECRETS OF KEEPING THE RED HOT ANIMAL LUST IN YOUR RELATIONSHIP—FORMER PORN QUEEN BARES ALL!"

These may be suitable to pass the time in the grocery store checkout line but to make their suggestions work in real life you'd need a 34-hour day, a winning lottery ticket, the body of a Russian gymnast, the creativity of a science fiction writer and a beachfront home in Malibu.

You see, marriage is a commitment, as Phil, Oprah, Geraldo, Sally Jesse, Maury, Joan, Ray Bob, Gunther and Eunice (consult your local listings for days and times) will be glad to tell you. It is a sacred bond between two adults who promise to love, honor and cherish one another, even after their body parts begin to sag, wrinkle and cease to function properly.

Unfortunately, it's only *after* the walk down the aisle that the reality of being locked together in Holy matrimony sets in. You must learn to put up with all your spouse's quirks, peculiarities and relatives. If she's a light sleeper, he almost certainly will grind his teeth in bed. If he likes things around the house "just so," she most certainly will be the kind who lets four weeks of dishes stack up in the sink so she can "do them all at once and get it over with."

This is all part of Mother Nature's little plan; and thank goodness for that, because it keeps life interesting. It makes us aware of the beautiful uniqueness in all of us. It gives us something to complain to our friends about over cocktails after work, and it keeps the needy children of divorce attorneys from having to struggle through life without sports cars and six-figure trust funds.

1

How to Survive the Wedding

Wedding Bell Blues

Well, you've spent months planning for this wedding, haven't you? And it *damn well better be perfect*. After all, isn't this the day you've been dieting for your entire life? You've spent a small fortune on the perfect attire and a large fortune on your good pals Jenny Craig, Richard Simmons and Jane Fonda. Not to mention long months you spent pounding away on the treadmill at Workout World at 6:00 every morning, flipping through *Bride's Magazine* and dreaming of glazed jelly doughnuts.

You've spent a solid week driving back and forth from the airport picking up out-of-town relatives you haven't seen since you were six years old. You barely know these people but not to worry; you'll have plenty of time to get acquainted with them because they'll be too cheap to get a motel room and will spend the week in your apartment. They'll empty your refrigerator, rearrange your furniture, offer you plenty of helpful advice about your wedding plans and keep your bathroom rug soaked from constant showering (which, strangely enough, will not seem to make them smell any better).

Once the hall has been rented, the minister called, the church filled with flowers, friends and organ music, you are ready to walk down the aisle into a new life of wedded bliss. It's *your* fairy tale, damnit, and all fairy tales end this way. The handsome prince kisses the fair maiden and they ride off into the sunset in a pumpkin carriage drawn by a couple of dwarfs and eight tiny reindeer.

Or something like that.

Goin' to the Chapel of Luv

Unfortunately, dreams of romance and magic kisses can, and do, go awry. Your bubble may very well burst when you find out your spouse's dad has hired Eddie Zeromsky and His Teutonic Tootlers' Oom Pah Band instead of the string quartet you expected. Or, when the groom drinks three bottles of warm champagne, tells his new mother-in-law she walks like a wounded water buffalo, makes a pass at the maid of honor and tells a joke over the PA system that involves three sorority girls and a donkey. Or, when the photographer accidentally exposes three quarters of the photographs from the church.

These things happen.

And so, you end up weeping in the corner of the banquet hall and collapsing, from exhaustion, embarrassment, cramped feet (because of those stupid $150 shoes you bought) and the fact that you've eaten no solid food for three weeks.

This is the moment when your mother will tromp over to you (like a wounded water buffalo) and say in an I-Told-You-So voice, "I told you not to marry that bum!" It's also about this time the groom's pals will gather in the parking lot to cheer, as the man of the hour attempts to break the nude, outdoor, no-hands beer chugging record.

Is this any way to start a marriage? Is your entire life together going to be an out-of-control nightmare? Well, probably.

But, hey, everybody's wedding is like this! Someone's crazy uncle always gets drunk and paws a bridesmaid and causes a fistfight. The deejay always plays "Mony, Mony" even after you slip him an extra twenty not to, and the groomsmen always cart the groom off to the men's room to dry shave his body hair. What would a wedding be without these and other good natured hi-jinks?

Will You Still Love Me Tomorrow?

After the VFW guys kick you out of the hall so they can set up for Bingo Night, you can escort each other to your luxurious suite for a night of wild passion. You're both better off, however, if you put the passion on hold, until the groom stops bleeding and throwing up.

In the not too distant past, however, the honeymoon night was a time-honored ritual in which the virgin bride, the defloweree, spent hours primping in the bathroom while the nervous groom, the deflowerer, fidgeted in bed, trying to remember all the good sexual advice his more experienced buddies had given him at the bachelor party. ("Most important thing to remember is to moan and sigh. Moan and sigh, I tell ya, ya can't do it enough!")

When the young bride returned, resplendent in a demure pink nightie, the lights were turned off, there was forty-eight seconds of fumbling in the dark, (and moaning and sighing) and, in nine months, a baby.

Were this a simpler, more gentle and refined age, I could spend a few moments here explaining how a couple's first night together should be a time of innocence, intimacy and discovery; a time when a young woman could turn to her young man and say, "You want me to do *what*?!" A time when a young couple could revel in the newness of love. Now, of course, I realize that you've been reveling like prairie dogs since your third date when you both got smashed on margaritas and woke up on the floor of her best friend's apartment wondering where your clothes were, where your car was and, scariest of all, who in the hell was this person snoring under the coffee table wearing your bra on his head? So I guess I can skip the talk about what the Mommy bird and the Daddy bird do to make a baby bird.

No, your honeymoon night will undoubtedly be spent at an airport hotel in a $300-a-night luxury suite in which you will spend about 76 minutes total. You will arrive from the wedding reception exhausted, collapse into bed and try to sleep despite two quarts of warm champagne fermenting in your stomach with the chicken Kiev, despite the fact that your plane leaves in three hours and you can't remember where you put the tickets, and despite the fact that 747s keep landing on the run-way twenty feet outside your window every six minutes.

Still, the honeymoon night is supposed to be a special one, so, if you can manage to stay awake, at least make a pass at your spouse. Oh, and don't forget to moan and sigh.

10 Things to Do on Your Honeymoon Night: For Men

1. Pass out in the tub.

2. Check ESPN for the sports wrap-up.

3. Check the cable for dirty movies.

4. Barf.

5. Open gifts and hopelessly mix up gifts and cards.

6. Order more booze from room service.

7. Remove mysterious stains from tux by showering in it.

8. Drink with your groomsmen at the hotel bar.

9. Drink with the bartender at the hotel bar after all your groomsmen have gone home.

10. Try to figure out why your wife is crying.

10 Things to Do on Your Honeymoon Night: For Women

1. Call your mother crying.

2. Call your best friend crying.

3. Sigh deeply and say, "Oh, nothing" when your husband asks, "What's wrong?"

4. Pass out on the bed.

5. Search for diaphragm.

6. Search for plane tickets.

7. Search for the annulment clause in pre-nuptial agreement.

8. Check the cable for a rerun of an old sappy movie.

9. Order the entire dessert menu from room service.

10. Try to figure out why you're crying.

Alone at Last

Your honeymoon is a once in a lifetime ... well, twice in a lifetime ... well, you may actually honeymoon a half dozen times before you die, but that doesn't mean you should take this trip any less seriously! Before you make any decisions, you must consult with a travel planning professional. Travel planning professionals are bored junior college dropouts who learned how to use the computer programs which airline reservationists use to book flights. They are highly qualified to arrange a vacation for you that will fulfill all your travel needs and that will get them out of the office in time to get their nails done before lunch.

When considering honeymoon destinations, you must decide what it is you each want to do during your vacation time. Are you sightseers? Do you enjoy sports? Do you like beach weather, or are you a skiing fanatic? Whatever destination you choose, you can be sure that your spouse will want to go somewhere completely different than you do. Not to worry! Choose the destination *you* prefer and let your spouse have the pleasure of blaming you for a miserable honeymoon for the remaining days of your marriage.

The honeymoon is very often the first opportunity a couple has to really spend some quality time together. Even couples who have lived together for years do not know true intimacy until they vacation together. Living together means you share a bathroom, the closets and the Mr. Coffee® machine. Hell, you probably only see each other for twenty minutes in the morning and an hour or two at night. Even on the weekends.

But when you vacation together, you will be stuck with each other for *24 fun-filled hours a day*. You will discover all sorts of new and wonderful things about each other. You wives may learn that you are married to a man who disappears into the bathroom at 9:22 every morning with the sports section, precisely 14 minutes after his first cup of coffee, and is gone for exactly 18 minutes each time. You may also discover that each and every time this man sits down, he makes a sound like a long sigh and a grunt, which sounds something like, "Aaaaaaaghnrrghshooo." You may find that he makes a phlegmy throat-clearing noise, each time he begins a sentence. You may find that he looks at his watch every ten minutes or so and says things like "Hmmm, 4:52 already." You may find that you want to strangle him.

And you husbands perhaps will notice things about your gal that you had previously been blind to. You may find that even though you've been sleeping together for years, your wife has been careful to never let you get a full view of her butt. You probably often wondered why she backed out of the room when she was naked, didn't you? Well, there is no concealing it anymore. Your new wife may also display a penchant for knick-knack buying. You may end up lugging home ashtrays, T-shirts, colorful, native pottery, posters, basketry, ceramic statues of Greek love gods, tiny hula dolls, sunglasses, beach umbrellas and fifty pairs of shoes. And that's just if you go to Niagra Falls. If you go to Mexico or Europe, you may have to charter a plane to get all your stuff home.

When the Honeymoon Is Over

So the honeymoon is over. And all you've got to show for it are peeling shoulders and four rolls of overexposed 35 mm film of Mexican children selling swaths of dyed burlap for 50 bucks a pop to tourists who think they're buying colorful native folk art. For the past several weeks you've been the center of attention. You've received dozens of gifts and piles of cash. You've had parties thrown in your honor. You've participated in a joyous religious spectacle; and you've been the subject of speeches, toasts and well-wishes from your friends and family.

But all that has now come to an end. Your friends are back to their own worries, your co-workers couldn't care less about your slides of Cancún, your boss has dumped a three-week backlog of paperwork on your desk and your family is so sick of you they don't want to see you until the next major holiday. (And then only if you're carrying an expensive gift.) Yes, the party is definitely over.

It's just the two of you now, alone together, staring dumbly across the breakfast table into each other's sleep-gunk encrusted eyes, both thinking the same loving thought: "I've got to wake up to *this* for the next 50 years?" Yes, you've now officially entered the Monday morning of your marriage, and it may not be a pretty sight.

Now that you're married, you will be discovering a whole slew of things about your spouse that you never knew before. Things that your beloved partner-for-life felt necessary to hide, but no longer does. You men will find that your wife owns 348 bras, and likes to wash and hang all of them over the shower curtain rod at the same time. You women may find that your heretofore polite and mannerly husband, now seems to think it pleasant to apply athlete's foot ointment at the dinner table.

Do not despair! This sort of behavior is to be expected and even encouraged! You want your spouse to know that you are so comfortable and happy with your union that you no longer feel you need to put any effort toward being an attractive, or even vaguely recognizable, human being. Share this good feeling with your spouse by proudly flaunting your various flaws. "See this, honey?" you might say while squeezing a wobbling, dimpled hunk of thigh flesh. "This is cellulite! It's never going to go away, and neither am I!"

You can quit going to the health club, start having fried pork sausage for breakfast everyday and stop clipping those little cauliflower-shaped skin tags that grow in your armpits. What the hell! You're married now!

Ten Ways to Tell When
the Honeymoon Is Over: For Husbands

1. She plops down on the toilet while you're brushing your teeth.

2. She starts wearing big, white cotton underwear instead of lacy, French-cut panties.

3. She uses your razor.

4. She buys condoms without blushing.

5. She lets her "bikini line" advance untrimmed, once bikini season is over.

6. She doesn't shave her legs in the winter, either.

7. You fall asleep without making a pass at her and she doesn't feel hurt. She'd rather sleep, too.

8. She comes to bed with skin care system products smeared all over her face.

9. She takes her mother's side in an argument.

10. She eats a quart of ice cream straight from the carton in front of you without apology or explanation. And, without offering you any.

Ten Ways to Tell When the Honeymoon Is Over: For Wives

1. He farts in bed.

2. He asks you to clip the hairs in his ears.

3. He uses your toothbrush and you don't mind.

4. He doesn't put the Sunday paper back in order for you after he's read it.

5. He buys tampons without blushing.

6. He forgets to remember the anniversary of the day you met—and you do, too.

7. He takes the last slice of pizza.

8. He schedules plans around your period, which he knows as well as you do.

9. He quits pretending to like your "eccentric" Uncle Ed.

10. He no longer holds the car door for you on "dates," and prefers to sit in the car honking the horn while you get ready.

2

How to Survive Living Together

Eek! A Spouse!

In the olden days of "Leave It to Beaver" and "Father Knows Best," young, single people lived with their parents until they married. This arrangement allowed courtship to take place under the watchful eyes of older and wiser folks and assured that sex would only occur during the four guilt-filled panicky minutes before curfew in the backseats of cars parked at the old ball field.

Nowadays, kids move out of their parents' homes some time after sixth grade, explaining, as they pack up their Nintendo® cartridges and Anthrax CDs, that they need "their independence" and want to "find out about the real world." What this means is that they want a place to have sex that doesn't have a stick shift. Of course, they'll still want meals and laundry privileges—they don't want to break away too quickly.

Chances are that you have lived on your own for years and so has your spouse. You each arrange the silverware drawer in your own way, you each have a different idea of what "clean" really means and you each have a sneaking suspicion the other has truly disgusting and horrible bathroom habits.

What this means is that most of your really nasty fights will not be about things like religion or politics, but about who left a glob of toothpaste on the bathroom sink to harden to a shiny, marble smooth finish. That's the downside. The upside is that not only will you be able to have sex in the comfort of your own home, but you'll have someone there all time who is not only allowed to have sex with you but is *actually legally and morally obligated to do so*. Of course, this will take all the excitement out of doing it, so you'll probably need some way to spice things up a bit. Try doing it in the backseat of your car near the old ball field.

Your Place or Mine?

Some lucky couples will be able to afford to buy their first home before they marry, thus pairing up the two largest traumas a human will ever face: marriage and dealing with a real estate closing. These couples have a 94% chance of divorce, but at least they have a home to fight over.

Luckily, this is not a problem most newlyweds face. Most newlyweds will have to decide whose apartment to live in. Should he have to live in her apartment because she spent all that money on ducky drapes, ducky shelf paper, ducky place mats and ducky hand towels? Or does it mean that she should live in his apartment because it's close to the golf course and overlooks the apartment complex's pool? After all, he spent a great deal of money on new clubs and those high-powered, able-to-read-the-label-on-a-bikini-top-at-250-yards binoculars.

Some couples live together before marriage to test if their relationship has the kind of staying power required for a good marriage and to see if they can stand each other when, after a fight, there's no place to go to escape.

Couples who live together and respect, admire, support and love one another as equals before marriage forget that the true meaning of the marriage certificate is that *you are now the property of your spouse.* For example, a man who loved a woman because of her outgoing, social nature will want to lock her in his home now that she's his private property. A woman who loved a generous man will now see him as wasteful and foolish and demand an account of every penny he spends.

It is the nature of ownership to do these things. The only thing I can suggest is that you draw up divorce papers with fill-in-the-blanks for names and dates and hang them on the refrigerator door as a constant threat. This should create enough uncertainty about the stability of your marriage to keep you treating each other like adults.

Bathroom Etiquette

There are those people who feel that it is acceptable, after marrying, to sit on the toilet while carrying on a conversation, while a spouse is in the tub, while using the phone, and while the door is open. This is particularly true of men and women who have been in the service, or have gone through an Outward Bound program. These people like to tell stories of "roughing it." They might say things like: "Why, I was in the woods for a week with eight people and no toilet paper. Hell, we used branches and leaves. Got to know each other *real* well, I'll tell ya." You do not really want to know your spouse this well. Trust me on this.

Anyone who plops down on the toilet seat and remarks on a particularly satisfying bowel movement should not later express surprise that the "magic" has gone out of the marriage.

It is important when sharing a bathroom to remember Mom's good old-fashioned advice: "Put things back the way you found them." That means that hunks of nostril hair should not be left in the sink, toilet paper rolls should not be left empty and mirrors should be cleaned of toothpaste splatters (and whatever else you've splattered on there, too). The air quality should be returned to normal, as well. That's what industrial strength air freshener is for.

Ultimately, there is the "toilet seat" question that apparently has been plaguing Americans for decades. That is, if you believe all the desperate "Lifestyle" section newspaper columnists who bring it up twice a year when they tire of writing about their own divorce or about a spunky Mom who bets her kids they can't go without watching TV for a year.

The question: Does the toilet seat belong up or down?

The answer: Neither.

The *whole lid* goes down, you uncouth pigs! It's nobody's business what you were doing in the bathroom before they got there. Whether you were going number one or number two, whether you were testing to see how you'd look with your hair parted on the other side or whether you were plucking rogue hairs from around your nipples, *put the lid down after you flush*. It keeps the mystery in your marriage.

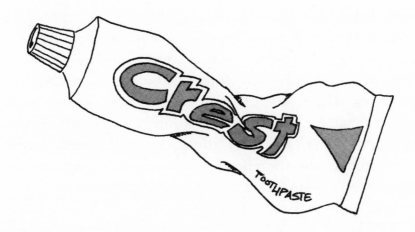

The Space Program

Once the decision of where to begin your new life together has been made, you will be faced with all sorts of niggling little difficult-to-sort-out dilemmas common to people who have moved in together and are discovering for the first time how horrifying it is to step barefoot onto a shag carpet full of toenail clippings which, until recently, have been attached to somone else's toes. Those of you who have lived in fraternity houses for any period of time have a distinct advantage in dealing with these problems, having already faced, and in a sick way enjoyed, much worse.

Dividing closet space, bathroom shelves and chores is a simple matter of allowing the wife to take all she needs. If you're very lucky, she may allow you a drawer. A small one, anyway. She's got five times as many clothes as you, three times as many "toiletries." The number of lotions, creams, masques and elixirs that a woman can smear, spread, dab and rub onto her various body parts is almost infinite. You may soon find yourself shaving in the kitchen using the reflective side of the toaster for a mirror. That's what a real man does, if he wants to get to work on time!

It takes time for a woman to figure out the exact combination of gooey stuff to smear on herself everyday. The kind of makeup a woman wears each day depends on her general coloring, the time of day, the season, the color of her clothes, her astrological sign, the temperature, the lighting, the Dow Jones Industrial average and the image she is attempting to create for that day. Also it depends on how much stuff she has left from that makeover session she got last month. The one that changed her from a workaday drudge into the hip, sprightly, together woman she is now. Which *you* didn't notice. Which is the real reason she stays in the bathroom for an hour forcing you to shave your chin around the General Electric logo and drink coffee out of your shaving mug.

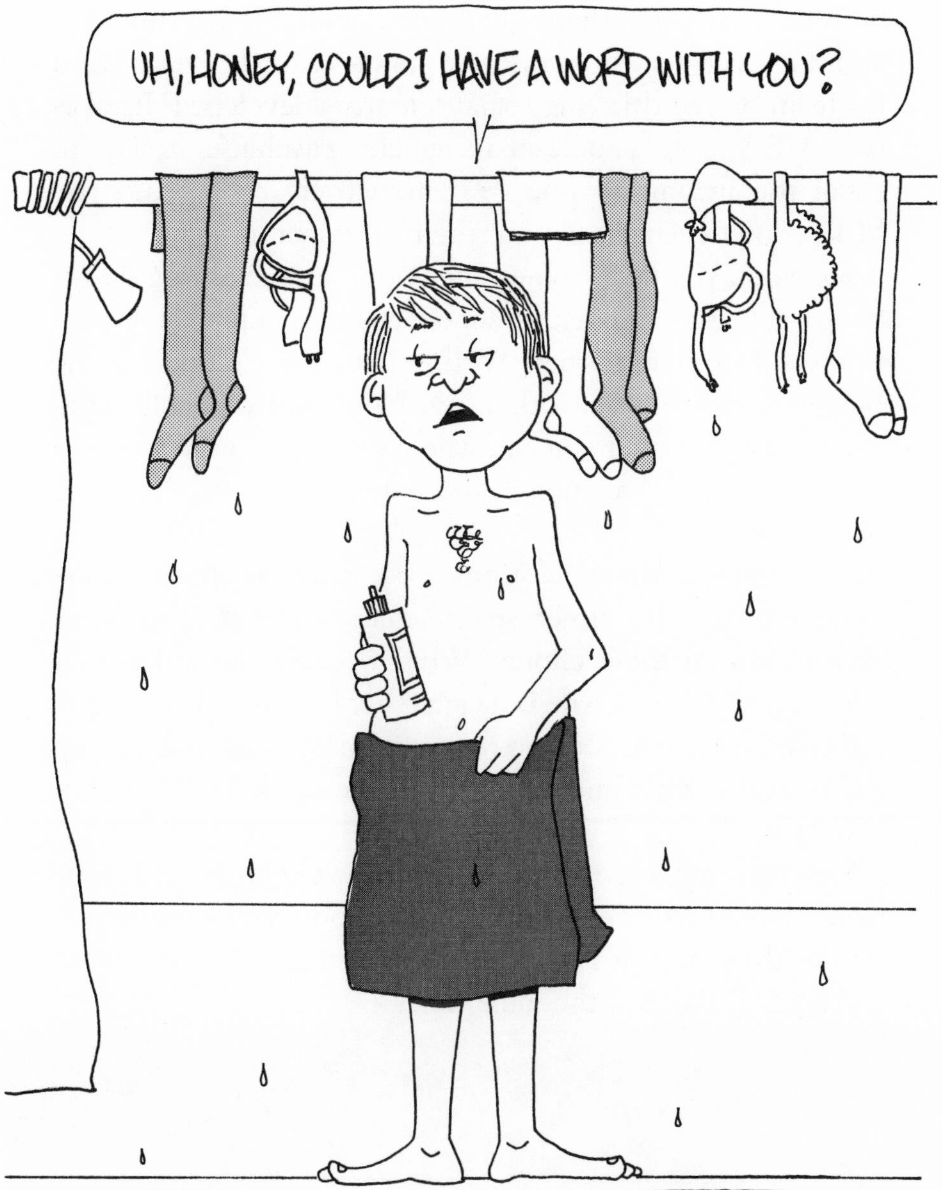
UH, HONEY, COULD I HAVE A WORD WITH YOU?

Dirty Dishes Done Dirt Cheap

Now, what about those chores? In most marriages today both partners work, thanks to modern, enlightened thinking, and the success of the economic policies Ronald Reagan and his team of free-thinking social scientists developed. It takes two MBA-level middle-management paychecks today to equal the income of one 1978 french fry cook. And you MBA's don't even get to wear the little paper hat.

So, when you both come home after an exhausting day of lying to clients, threatening suppliers and gossiping about co-workers, who fixes dinner? Well, usually the Colonel, or the Burger King® or some other royal provider of cholesterol. That's easy. But after you eat, who cleans up? And who vacuums? And dusts? And mops? And waters the plants? And does the laundry?

The answer to these questions is as easy as the answer to the "who gets all the closet space" question. And the same. Women do all these chores. Why? Because the only other option available to a wife is nagging her husband until he gets up, looks in the bathroom at the green mold-beast crawling up the shower curtain and says "What's wrong? It looks okay in here to me!"

Men are simply too ill-equipped in the chore-doing department to do anything but wreak havoc on your entire house. It's not their fault. It's genetic. Like a woman's ability to drive and apply makeup at the same time.

10 Chores That Men Can Do

1. Barbecue.

2. Take out the trash.

3. Get firewood.

4. Adjust the thermostat. Downward of course, ("Put on a sweater, you think electricity grows on trees?")

5. Clean out gutters. (Men find any chore that requires a hose fun. What would Freud say?)

6. Wash and wax cars. (See hose reference above.)

7. Be in charge of the remote. (You may never see a movie from beginning to end again.)

8. Anything with tools.

9. Change window screens. (A twice a year job.)

10. Hook up electrical equipment.

Stereo Types

There are myriad differences between men and women, not the least of which is the ability to hear. Both sexes can hear, but they each hear differently. A woman can hear the breathing of a sleeping baby in an upstairs bedroom of a house in the next zip code. Strangely enough, this same woman will be unable to hear the snap, crackle and pop of an ancient phonograph needle as it bounces and skitters down the grooves of a 45 rpm record.

To a man, music is the soundtrack to life. Only a male would buy a $500 car and put a $4,500 stereo system in it. A man's stereo system and his choice of music define him. He will sleep on a mattress on the floor, drink from old jelly jars and eat off paper plates, but he will always have enough money for another obscure and complex stereo component. You see, not only can he hear frequencies that women and dogs are unable to hear, but his ears can withstand volumes that would make a woman want to hide her head in a clothes hamper. To hear the latest "Acid Puke Orchestra" album a man needs a CD player, an amplifier, a pre-amplifier, a reel-to-reel tape deck, a turntable, an $800 stylus, an equalizer and a pair of speakers slightly smaller than your refrigerator. He will stand between these speakers at a distance of sixteen inches, turn the volume up until the neighbor's windows rattle and say, "Hmm, I just don't like the signal-to-noise-ratio on this recording."

Yes, music is important to a man. He will stay up until 4 A.M. on the night before you take a long car trip mixing just the right songs for a "Road Tape." It will contain songs appropriate for driving. He will also have a "Mellow Tape" for rest stops, a "Rockin' Tape" to help him stay awake during nighttime driving, a "Gas Station Tape" for fill-ups, and a "Want to Get Lucky Tape" for when ... well, you figure it out.

A woman is likely to bring to her marriage a portable record player with the faces of the Brady Bunch on the inside of the lid and a round plastic carrying case filled with scratchy 45s that she and her friends listened to during slumber parties in junior high school. She will also own six albums, each of which represents a milestone in her life. One will be the soundtrack album to *West Side Story* (first exposure to "Romeo and Juliet" movie theme), a Jackson Five album (first boy-girl dance), a Barry Manilow album (first boyfriend), a Neil Diamond album (second boyfriend), Pink Floyd's *Dark Side of the Moon* (first hippie boyfriend) and Barbra Streisand's *Greatest Hits* (to sing along with defiantly after breaking up with boyfriends).

Some advice for newly married women: Don't play the Barbra Streisand record on his stereo system unless you consult a divorce attorney first.

It's a Gas, Gas, Gas

Until you marry and begin living with your spouse, you may not be aware that he or she farts. When dating, most couples wish to impress one another with what swell, cultured folks they are and, since nothing goes further to douse a romantic mood than a raucous, rumbling fart, most people find a way to squelch their natural emissions.

Once the banns are read, however, the true content of your spouse's colon may be revealed to you in all its glory. Women who were previously sweet smelling and demure may now revel in the casualness of marriage and feel free to unleash trumpet-like blasts of air with astonishing frequency.

Some men enjoy playing "Fart, Fart, Who Hid the Fart?," a husband bedtime game in which he quietly looses large quantities of flatus beneath the covers, so as to surprise his unsuspecting wife with a flap of the comforter.

How does one tell, then, before marriage, if one's fiancé is a closet flatulence fiend? Try taking your intended to a Mexican restaurant, where you can fill your significant other with spicy food. Later, when you're at home, and the chili relleno has had a chance to percolate for awhile, engage him or her in a wild tickling match. This should be enough to loosen the sphincter of someone with the constitution of Princess Diana. Using this method will allow you to get an idea of what kind of smells you'll be living with for the rest of your life. Do it before your wedding! Most states will not allow divorce on the grounds of nasal cruelty.

3

How to Survive Your Friends and Relatives

Jumping into the Gene Pool

One of the most common delusions you may have as a newly married person is that you are marrying the one human being on the face of this earth who will make your life whole and perfect. You are wrong! This is folly of the most damaging sort. The fact is, you are marrying several hundred people, some of whom you haven't even met yet. Some of whom are actually dead. These human beings are called in-laws. You see, you are not marrying a human being at all. You are marrying a family tree.

Maybe you haven't given much thought to dealing with the family of your beloved. Maybe you even think you like most of them. Maybe you haven't yet spent an entire Thanksgiving day trapped in a musty rec room with them, immersed in a discussion of whether stuffing should be cooked inside the turkey or out. Maybe you haven't yet had the eerie pleasure of meeting your spouse's hillbilly cousins from West Virginia, Aunt Eunice and Uncle Ray Bob, whose children are also your spouse's aunts and uncles, (if you know what I mean, and I think you do). In fact, you may have the distinct impression that "Dueling Banjos" is playing somewhere every time one of their kids comes into the room.

Your first instinct may be to toss raw meat and cans of Pabst Blue Ribbon® beer at these people and then flee the area. However, this is impolite and you'll mess up your carpeting besides. Remember, strange as it may seem as you look at them scratching hidden skin rashes and spitting tobacco juice into your houseplants, in-laws can be the source of tremendous information about your spouse's early years. They can regale you for hour upon hour with tales of bedwetting, acne, embarassing brushes with the law and more. The may even have photos.

Just Call Us "Mom & Pop"

Perhaps you have spent a good deal of time with your spouse's folks during your courtship and engagement and you don't find them at all repugnant. If this is the case, try to remember that you felt this way *before* they were related to you! Once you've tied the knot, seemingly normal, mild-mannered folk undergo a horrific metamorphosis.

You haven't yet had the pleasure of sitting through your father-in-law's lecture on the history of indoor plumbing, which he gives after every holiday meal when the Gallo kicks in. Your mother-in-law will now be calling ten times a day "just to touch base," and, when she does, your spouse will remain trapped on the phone with her, unable to escape because it would "hurt her feelings, and you know how sensitive she's been since the hip replacement."

But, don't despair. You can learn from these folks. Watch them as they sit in their matching plaid recliners. See how he stabs at the TV with his remote control, changing channels so fast that the shows only register subliminally in your brain? Notice how he adjust his hearing aid and hollers at the play-by-play man to quit mumbling and speak up? See how she sits in her chair, sipping sherry, knitting and humming, letting out little ladylike farts and covering the noise with little ladylike coughs? Notice how her orange, knee-high support hose stick out from under her twenty-year-old house dress? Did you watch them both fall asleep, snoring and whistling in their chairs at precisely 9:30 P.M.?

Take note, folks. That's you in thirty years.

GOOD NEWS, "SON", WE'RE STAYING AN EXTRA WEEK! THE REST OF THE BAGS ARE IN THE CAR.

Relatively Speaking: Understanding the Mysterious Language of In-Laws

You've been with your spouse long enough now to realize that what he/she says is frequently not exactly what he/she means. This is what psychologists like to call "dysfunctional communication" or, in layman's terms, "messing with your mind." Your in-laws play this game, too. Where the hell do you think your spouse got it from?

Here are some of the phrases you can expect to hear from your in-laws, and their literal translations.

When they say:
"We'd love to see more of you."
They mean:
"You've stolen our child from us."

When they say:
"We're expecting you for the holidays."
They mean:
"Pack a bag. You won't be sneaking out of here after the football game this year."

When they say:
"Family life is wonderful, isn't it?"
They mean:
"So, am I going to have a grandchild before I die, or what?"

When they say:
"Eat up! You're just skin and bones!"
They mean:
"Learn to cook, you're starving my baby!"

When they say:

"Goodness, you've done so much with this house."

They mean:

"I see the roach problem has finally cleared up some."

When they say:

"How's work going?"

They mean:

"My daughter could have married that rich doctor."

When they say:

"We'd be happy to sit with the kids."

They mean:

"We'd be happy to fill the kids with ice cream and candy and let them stay up late, undoing in one night all the discipline you've tried to instill in the past few years. After all, they're your problem now."

When they say:

"We don't want to be a burden."

They mean:

"Reach for your checkbook, baby."

It's *Such* a Wonderful Life

Now that you're married, you'll want to begin observing your own special holiday traditions as a couple. Start by decorating your car, because once you're hitched, all your holidays will be spent rattling along the U.S. interstate system arguing about whether or not booze is an appropriate gift for Uncle Buddy, considering that last year he got tanked up and ate your nephew's pet goldfish, Jaws, while demonstrating an old fraternity prank.

Another fabulous holiday tradition is the annual "Whose Parents Are We Going to Spend Christmas with This Year, Honey?" fight which is almost always won by the spouse who is most deftly able to employ the classic, passive-aggressive "Boy Am I Going to Make You Feel Guilty Now" argument.

The winner of this fight is inevitably the spouse who holds the holidays closest to her heart. I say her heart because, let's face it, we're talking about the wives here, aren't we? To men, Christmas is just an excuse to have another college bowl game. Of course, when you are married to a woman who takes Christmas seriously, you, too, will be required to get into the old Christmas spirit, whether you like it or not. You'll be shopping for presents in July, putting the tree up just after Halloween and decorating the old domicile with assorted plastic Santas, Rudolphs, wise men, shepherds, angels and enough blinking lights for a DC-10 to attempt a landing on your roof at night. *Feliz navidad*, amigo.

And, if you don't go to *her* parents' house on Christmas, she'll spend the entire holiday in the corner of the rec room nibbling stale sugar cookies from a TV tray, sipping egg nog and watching eighteen straight showings of *It's a Wonderful Life*.

Ask her what the matter is and she'll just sigh a tiny Joan of Arc sigh and say, "Oh, nothing, it's just that at our house we always open presents on Christmas Day instead of *spoiling everything* by opening them on Christmas Eve. But don't worry, I'll be fine."

How to Have Happy Holidays
—for Men Only

Observing the holidays is something that all women hold close to their hearts. It is because they are the tradition-keepers of our culture. It is because they are the nurturers of our family life. It is because they like a constant supply of gifts. My advice for men: Go to a local mall every year on January 2nd. Buy appropriate gifts and cards for each of the following holidays. Stack these gifts in your office in order and check on them once a month.

Valentine's Day

This is the big one, guys. She expects a card, and jewelry. Earrings are always nice. And no Far Side® cards! Find the gooiest, sappiest piece of sentimental garbage you can. Get them by the dozen and trade with your married buddies. *Do not blow this holiday*. It is the Super Bowl of holidays, and if you screw up, you will be facing months of "Wrong? What could be wrong? Just because I'm married to the most thoughtless, hardhearted, dirt sucking weasel on earth, doesn't mean there's something WRONG!"

Easter

Not a biggie. You can slide by with flowers. Order them in January and have them shipped to her at the office.

Mother's Day

If your wife is also a mommy, you've got to not only come up with something for her from you, but also something for her from the little tykes. And don't bother with that breakfast in bed routine. That only works in orange juice commercials and television sitcoms. She knows she's going to have to clean up after you. Get her a nice silk scarf. Don't worry about taste or style, she's going to return it anyway, just to see how much you spent. And don't forget your own mom! And hers! Yes, you get it from four sides on this festive occasion.

July Fourth

Yes, you've got to come through today, too. Not necessarily with gifts, but be prepared to man the grill and barbecue animal flesh, or take the family to the fireworks. It's a tradition, and traditions are important. If you try to spend the day watching a ball game you will be reminded of it until ...

Labor Day

(Repeat above.)

Halloween

A card is in order here, gentlemen, and a small gift. Anything black will do—a skirt, a sweater or a blouse. The more money you spend, the more leverage you'll have during your argument about whether or not you have to wear that embarrassing bunny outfit and go to that stupid costume party.

Thanksgiving

You get a buy on this one, boys. A card will do and perhaps a couple of trips to the grocery store for food and beer. Then, eat like a pig and pass out in front of a football game. It's traditional! Yes, Thanksgiving is a man's holiday. Thank God! You'll need the rest before ...

Christmas

Choose here from each of the four basic gift groups: clothes, jewelry, fragrance and cash. A balanced selection is important. 'Tis the season to be debt ridden.

Her Birthday

Another monster. We're looking at a card, a gift and a night on the town. And I'm not talking about taking her to a tractor pull, guys. Birthdays are for the whole—white tablecloth, candlelight, expensive wine and sneering maitre d'—schmeer. Flowers are a must and jewelry is strongly recommended. Hopefully, when you bought the earrings for her on Valentine's Day you were smart enough to purchase the matching necklace, which you can lay on her now. She will be impressed by your taste and style, which you can further enhance by also buying the matching bracelet and brooch for your ...

Anniversary

This is the big day. It was the most memorable day of your life, right? I know you rolled a perfect 300 game last year, but that's a different kind of memory. *It does not compare to the day you wed your lovely wife!* Again selections from the four major gift groups are in order, plus flowers, plus dinner, plus ... chin up here, men ... you've got to come through in the sack. Yes, not only do you have to come up with the gifts, you've got to make love to her as though you still enjoy it. Actually, if you come up with enough gifts, she might let you off the hook.

A note here about lingerie: She knows that it's more for you than it is for her, so don't bother.

Keeping Up with the Joneses

After your wedding, you'll find yourselves drawn less to your single friends and more toward your married ones. This is natural. Single people spend their time *doing* things. They go to parties, bars and shopping, as well as to theaters and ball games. They spend all their time thinking about having fun, which, now that you're married, is *just not important to you anymore*. You don't have time for such frivolous behavior! While you enjoy a great evening of re-papering the powder room with your honey, your buddies are stuck in some smoky room drinking beer, telling crude jokes and playing poker until all hours of the morning. Aren't they pathetic?

Let's face it, your single friends are jealous of you and your spouse. They envy the way you spend your evenings lounging around the house in sweat clothes rereading old magazines, flipping through TV channels and staring contentedly at one another. You are "cocooning" and you love it! Only another married couple would understand how much fun and excitement you now enjoy every day of your lives. This is why you must only go out with married people.

When you "date" another married couple, there is as much protocol to observe as when you were dating each other. Remember to always sit "boy-girl-boy-girl" so you can flirt with one another's spouse. This will give you the momentary illusion that there's the tiniest chance that you might not have to have sex with the same person for the rest of your life.

This rule applies everywhere but in the car, where the men should sit in the front seat and the women in the back. This way the men can talk about sports and cars, and the women can talk about clothes and how their needs aren't being met by their men.

"But, Honey, We're Just Good Friends"

There is no such thing as a friend of the opposite sex. You want to mess around, and you know it. So does your spouse. You're not fooling anyone. So just stop it.

Ex Marks the Spot

Morality being what it is today (that is, close to non-existent), you may be on marriage number two (or three, or four). Maybe each of you has been married before. Maybe there are kids, and step-kids, and ex-parents-in-law and ex-grandparents-in-law. Jeez, your life is a mess, isn't it?

During the courting and engagement period, you will come to know your spouse's ex through the colorful and detailed stories your spouse will tell about his/her ex's sexual shortcomings, personality flaws, questionable hygiene practices, inability to earn money and all-around undesirability. Tape record these reminiscences for later use, because after the wedding, that same ex, who was inconsiderate and rude in bed, in the bathroom and at family get-togethers—that same human who has been described to you as a near felon and who was only saved from a life of dissolution, shame and petty theft by the grace of your spouse—will suddenly be transformed by the miracle of *Marital Selective Memory* (MSM) into the kind of paragon of virtue whose shoes you are not fit to kneel before.

MSM is a wonderfully handy mental condition which allows you to conveniently forget things from your past that might be of concern to your new spouse. ("Honey, did I ever tell you about my third wife? Well, she's coming through town this week with the circus and she needs a place to stay. It'll only be for a month or so and the seals are just like pets. They hardly smell at all!")

Possibly, you will have a relationship with your ex. Or, your spouse's ex. Given the way things go in this movie-of-the-week world we live in, they may even get married to each other. Perhaps you'll all vacation together. In any case, it's important to maintain friendly relations with your spouse's ex. Because your spouse's ex is the one person in the whole world who knows exactly how to make your spouse crazy, which can come in very handy.

4

How to Survive in Bed

Frequency Modulation

The question most couples eventually ask each other in bed is usually not, "How good is it?" but, "How often are we gonna do it?" When you live alone, you can have sex any old time you like. The problem with having sex with someone *besides* yourself is that you have to consider *their* needs, too. Early in marriage, it is frequently the man who desires sex more often than the woman. He will grab, pinch, poke and fondle private parts constantly. Sometimes his wife's, too. This early "Passionate Period," or "Random Groping Period," may last as long as several weeks. After that, his interest may wane.

You see, men tend to marry a woman just like dear old Mom. This is why the physical side of a relationship goes straight downhill immediately after the wedding night. While it's true that most men would mount a Burmese spitting llama if they thought it would mean a sexual thrill, it's tough for a man to have randy ideas about the woman who toilet trained him.

While men experience a slackening off of sexual desire after marriage, women often experience a feeling of liberation. Once she's married, a woman often feels freed from the constraints of religion and morality which caused her to have guilt, shame and to confess to her clergyman about her various electronic vibrating appliances.

Unfortunately, men often find that violating these religious and moral constraints is much more exciting than the act itself. This means that women should not toss that vibrator in the trash just yet. As a matter of fact, it's smart to keep a fresh supply of batteries around, too.

Creating a Diversion

What is necessary to keep the spark alive sexually is a relearning of our sexual roles. Let's begin with the men. First of all, guys, women need to feel loved and desired if they are to get in the mood for sex. Grabbing your groin and hollering "Hey, honey, I'm horny as a hoot owl!" is not sufficient foreplay. Most women need a good deal of physical affection that—pay attention here, boys—*does not necessarily have to wind up in intercourse!* They want to be held, to cuddle and to play kissy-face. Now, after all this kissing and cuddling you probably *will* end up in the sack, but it is important to pretend that all the kissing and cuddling you're doing is inspired by warmth and affection for her, and that you're not just killing time until orgasm. It is important that you understand how to create this illusion, if you are going to connect fully with your wife, and if you ever want to get laid again.

Now, you women must remember that men are extremely visual creatures. Just because *you* think dressing in a nun's habit with a garter belt and stockings on underneath is sacrilegious does not mean that it's a bad thing. If it makes your husband happy for you to dress this way, smack his hands with a ruler and call him "a very, very, bad boy" then hey, where's the harm? Remember all the times he cuddled with you, when there was a perfectly good Division A college basketball game that he could have been watching on TV? If a man is not fulfilling your needs for intimacy, you must confront him.

This is a delicate, sensitive matter, so approach him when the two of you have a moment together. Perhaps in the intimacy of the marriage bathroom, when you're both free from the distractions of the coming day and he has a face full of shaving cream and can't interrupt you.

After the Thrill Is Gone

It is inevitable that boredom will begin to creep into your sex life, at some point. Usually when you realize, shortly after your honeymoon, that you are going to be having sex with the same person, the same way, in the same places and at the same times for the rest of your life! At this time, you will also realize that this person is always going to want you to lick his ear, even though it makes you think of ear wax and that this person is always going to wear those little golf socks to bed, because her feet get cold, despite the fact that the sight of a naked woman wearing little pink sockies who screams, "Oh, baby," takes a good deal of the magic out of the lovemaking for you.

It is vitally important to keep romance alive in a marriage. Set aside one night a week to have a "date" with your spouse. Do all those things you used to do together when you were still trying to decide whether or not you were going to sleep together. Go to the carnival, take a long walk on the beach, have a picnic in the country, browse antique stores, etc. Soon you'll realize that the reason you got married was so that you'd never have to do any of that again. Then you can go back to being bored with each other without feeling as though there was something missing from your lives.

Let's talk about unrealistic expectations, people! Love may make the world go 'round but it really comes in handy when your husband rolls over in bed and asks you if you could pop the pimple in the middle of his back that he just can't reach. It may be hard to rekindle the magic of romance and passion after such a request, but hell, there will probably come a day when you need him to pick up a box of tampons for you at the store, so it all evens out.

The Old Softy

Sometimes even the most virile of men can have an impotence problem. There is nothing abnormal about that. While women can fake it if they have to, a man's lack of desire is always quite apparent. It is crucial that a woman handle this situation with a gentle touch—so to speak. Here is a helpful list of things to say when your husband comes up a little short.

1. "It's no biggie, excuse the pun."

2. "It's okay, dear, I didn't feel like faking it tonight anyway."

3. "What's the matter, no lead in the old pencil?"

4. "I hear there's an operation for that now."

5. "Hand me my vibrator and that photo of Kevin Costner, will you?"

6. "Now what am I going to do for the next two and a half minutes?"

7. "Oh good, now we can see all of 'The Top Ten List.'"

8. "If you can't cut the mustard, you can still lick the jar."

9. "Dress up in my underwear. That always worked for my other lovers."

10. "So, we'll wait 'til next month."

The Pajama Game

Early in your marriage, when both spouses are still trying to impress each other, a wife will wear whatever makes her feel most attractive, to bed. She'll feel sexy; he'll feel sexy. As times goes by, however, he will discover that to his surprise, there is such a thing as *not feeling like doing it*. Eventually, the wife will realize that nothing she does is going to get him remotely interested in her anymore, and the truth is that she's not all that interested, herself. At some point, comfort, for women, will take precedence over appearance in bed.

A man, however, simply assumes that he's sexually appealing no matter what he wears to bed. Besides, what he wears to bed is a deeply ingrained behavior, that was taught to him early in life. Some men sleep in their jammies because that's what Mommy taught them to wear. Some men sleep in their holey, stained, all-American jockey shorts because that's what Uncle Sam taught them to wear in the service. Some men sleep naked because they read a dirty paperback in high school and that's what the stud in the book did. In any case, it's too late to do anything about it. If you don't find his jammies with the little rocket ships on them sexually attractive, he'll figure it's your problem.

Nonetheless, there's nothing that indicates the relative marital temperature as accurately as does what a wife wears to bed every night.

1st month
Nothing.

2nd month
Make up, garter belt, stockings.

3rd month
   Lacy camisole.

4th month
   Teddy.

5th month
   Sheer nighty.

6th month
   Flannel nighty.

7th month
   T-shirt.

8th month
   T-shirt and underwear.

9th month
   T-shirt, underwear and socks.

10th month
   T-shirt, underwear, socks and sweat pants.

11th month
   T-shirt, underwear, socks, sweat pants, skin cream and curlers.

12th month
   Nothing, but at this point, who cares?

You've Lost That Lovin' Feelin'

When you are newly married, and sex is still an interesting and exciting thing, a man will dedicate hours to the process of seduction and foreplay. He does this because he delights in the very touch and feel and smell of his lovely wife, because he adores her and wants to fulfill her every sexual desire and because he saw the Phil Donahue show entitled "Foreplay: For Men Only."

Unfortunately, as time goes by a man gets less and less interested in the preliminaries and more interested in the final act. This is due to physiological differences between men and women more than anything else. A man can become aroused, reach orgasm and be sound asleep in the time it takes a woman to unhook her bra.

This then is the companion list to "The Pajama Game." It seems that the time men are willing to spend on foreplay is directly linked to how a woman dresses for bed. Or maybe, how much care a woman puts into dressing for bed is directly linked to how much time her husband is willing to spend on foreplay. To follow is a list of the typical amounts and kinds of foreplay that you can expect during the early part of your marriage. Those of you who are living in sin will find that the decline in foreplay is less drastic because living together creates the illusion that you must still try to please your partner in bed. Eventually even that tiny ember of romance is squelched by the sands of time.

1st month
A three hour, candle-lit dinner by the fireplace with wine, flowers, slow dancing to Sinatra records, a sensuous strip tease, bubble bath and hot oil massage.

2nd month
Two hours of passionate necking, full body massages and that thing with the silk neck ties and the feather that you read about in the Kama Sutra.

67

3rd month

Two hours of necking and a back rub.

4th month

A half hour of necking and fondling.

5th month

A half hour of necking and fondling while viewing a sexually oriented video tape made especially for couples, with an interesting plot, believable dialogue and "soft core" sex.

6th month

Ten minutes of groping in front of "The Horny Housewives and Mailman Mike."

7th month

He watches "Horny Housewives" and wakes her up when he comes to bed.

8th month

He pats her on the rump.

9th month

He comes up behind her and unsnaps her bra.

10th month

He says, "Wanna do it?" and turns the TV off.

11th month

He says, "Wanna do it?" and leaves the TV on.

12th month

He wakes up with an erection and says, "Got one."

Bedtime Paper Dolls

Practice preparing yourself for the coming changes in your spouse's bedroom attire by dressing up the paper doll. Combine the articles of clothing in any way you like. Use your imagination! Have fun! Chances are, now that you're married, this will be as close as you'll get for awhile.

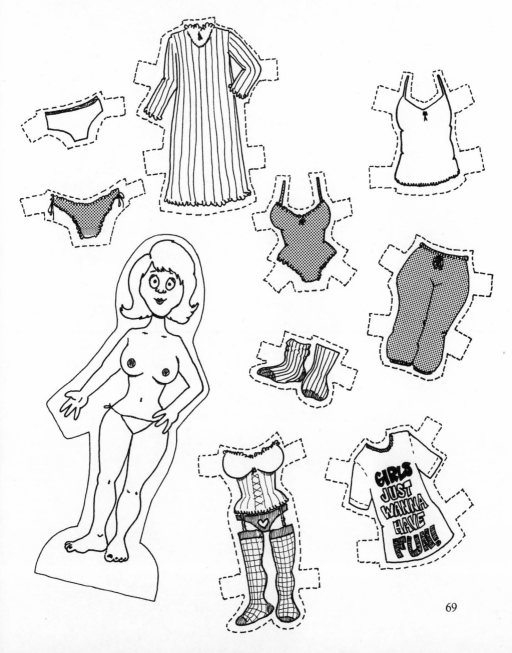

69

5

How to Survive
Each Other

Communication Breakdown

Some experts feel that it is communication, rather than having separate bathrooms, that is the key to a great marriage. What do they know? Communication is a concept that means something completely different to a man than it does to a woman. To a man, great communication means that he is able to nod his head and grunt at his wife with a mouth full of food and she will understand this to mean, "Great meat loaf, honey. Pass the ketchup."

Great communication to a woman means that her husband is able to intuitively know her every whim, fancy, desire, mood and where she is in her cycle. Great communication also means that he should say just the right thing, at just the right time, in just the right way, so as to make her feel just exactly the way she wants to feel, every time she wants to feel that way. This is why so many marital fights end with those famous words, "If you don't know what's wrong, I'm certainly not going to tell you." Most of the time when someone says these famous words, that person doesn't know what the hell he or she wants you to say either.

But that's not really the point. When your wife revs up her whining machine she doesn't want you to help her solve her little problems. She wants you to sit there and listen. Women must find whining to be a joyous, cathartic experience which is why they spend so much time doing it. It has nothing to do with you or the state of the world. It's automatic, like a cat's purr. The key to good marital communication is for the husband to develop the ability to look interested and alert while really watching TV or thinking about deer season. Seasoned veteran husbands are able to do this and even say "uh huh" and "yes, honey" once in awhile.

In general, women and men are physically much different creatures. A man is best able to hear and understand frequencies in the 24 to 67 hertz range of sound. Within this range fall sounds of sportscaster's voices, sounds of cars being wrecked and people being kicked in the groin with steel-toed boots in Steven Seagal movies, as well as the sound of a properly tuned automobile engine. Outside of his normal range of hearing are the sounds of a baby crying, his own snoring and, as you've already suspected, the female voice.

Women are unable to hear something as important as the score of a late night West Coast ball game on Sportscenter but can actually hear "marked down" price tags being stapled to skirts in a mall three miles away.

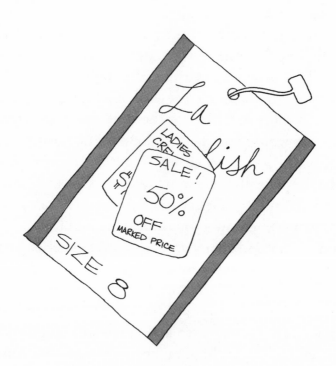

Feelings, Nothing More Than Feelings

Another important thing to remember about communication is that talking about your "feelings" is very important to women. They seem to have a creepy desire to know a man's every secret thought, fear and fantasy. Men are notoriously close-mouthed about their secret thoughts, fears, desires and fantasies for the simple reason that they know what those fantasies are and they fear jail.

Beware of your wife's efforts to uncover your feelings, men! Tell her a secret desire or fantasy and sure as shootin' some night, at a dinner party when she's pissed at you for paying too much attention to your boss' busty new trophy wife, she won't be able to resist the urge to hiss at you, "I suppose you'd love to get up in front of all *these* people in my lacy silk panties and dance the merengue with a flower in your teeth, wouldn't you?"

You see, feelings are not as important to a man as they are to a woman. Or important at all, really. Men don't get married so they can have someone with whom they can share their feelings. They get married *so they don't have to talk about their feelings ever again!*

This does not mean that men have no feelings, they do. Men weep openly, when it is proper to do so. Like at the end of *The Great Escape* when Steve McQueen can't jump his motorcycle over the barbed wire, or when watching a video of the final seconds of the 1980 U.S. Olympic Hockey Team's win over Russia.

However, just in case you men find yourselves unprepared in what could be an emotionally intimate moment with your wives, the following list might help you out.

P.S. I Love You:
10 Things to Say When She Asks,
"Do You Love Me?"

1. "Heck, I married you, didn't I?"

2. "Ungh."

3. "Sure, sure. Where's the remote control?"

4. "Define love."

5. "In what sense?"

6. "C'mere, baby, I'll show ya some love."

7. " Zzzzzzz."

8. "I took out the trash, didn't I?"

9. "Love is not the word for the way I feel about you, honey."

10. "What was the question?"

Marital Martial Arts

You will find, as you and your spouse divide chores, closets and time in charge of the TV remote, that you will have an occasional tiff. In a normal marriage you will only argue with your spouse about 87% of the time you are together. The rest of the time you will not have the energy. These little disagreements, called "spats," "arguments" or "divorce preliminaries," are healthy and normal as long as they are not allowed to develop into anything that results in injury.

The important thing to remember about fighting with your spouse is that there is no way for you to win. No matter what the fight is supposed to be about, it always comes down to this chilling realization: "This person I married is never going to behave the way I want them to. *Ever.*"

This does not mean that you should give up arguing with your spouse. Heavens, no. A good fight clears the air, burns calories and helps you get rid of excess crockery.

There are some important guidelines to observe when fighting. Women, never mention his mother. And men, remember that what you say to your wife in the heat of the moment is going to haunt you for the rest of your life. Women have tremendous power of recall when it comes to having their feelings hurt. It's kind of like your ability to remember baseball stats from the late 60s. A woman can not only remember every mean thing you ever say for the rest of her life, she can also remember the outfit she was wearing when you said it.

Keep this in mind and all your fights will be fair, healthy, loving discussions in which not too much property is destroyed and which give the neighbors something to talk about for awhile.

Joined at the Hip

For the first few months of your marriage you will go everywhere and do everything together. When your wife goes to the bathroom at a ball game with her friend, you husbands will feel pangs of jealousy. When your husband goes to his weekly softball game, you wives will still feel his arm about your waist like a phantom limb. Don't worry, these symptoms of infatuation will soon wear off. Where at first you were thrilled to hear your new husband refer to you as "my wife," you will soon scream at him, "I'm not anybody's wife, damnit! I'm my own person with my own needs, wants, goals, hopes and desires! And don't you forget it." It would be best if you did not do this in a crowded restaurant or theater.

There are, of course, events you will be expected to attend as a couple. Other people's weddings, for instance. Family outings and company events, too. If you try to attend a high school reunion without your spouse, she will know that you are hoping to rekindle an old flame and enjoy a little "nostalgia nookie." That's the only reason anyone ever goes to those things anyway. Lines like, "Oh, honey, you'd just be bored with all our reminiscing," sound just as insincere as they are. Besides, everybody else's spouse is going to be there hovering like a helicopter, so save your fantasies for another time.

Some women get so used to having their husbands in bed with them that they can't sleep unless they get a tape recording of his snoring. They also may hire someone to put icy feet on them in the middle of the night, pull the covers off every twenty minutes, fart loudly and continuously and walk noisily to the bathroom every two hours and flush the toilet.

The Argument Wheel

One of the most frequent disagreements a married couple will encounter occurs when one spouse would like to attend an event or party and the other would rather not. These can include company softball games, niece's piano recitals and various arcane religious milestones of various arcane relatives (baptisms, confirmations, bat mitzvahs, funerals, etc.)

To make this kind of fight easier, I've developed this simple psychological exercise. Begin at any space on the wheel and go round and round until you strangle each other or collapse from sheer exhaustion.

1. If you loved me, you'd go with me.

2. If you loved me, you wouldn't ask me to go with you.

3. But I always go with you to *your* things when I know *I* won't like it.

4. Yes, and you always ruin it for me when you do that.

5. So, you don't want me to be with you.

6. I do, but not if you're not going to have a good time.

7. But I enjoy it when *you* have a good time.

8. And I enjoy it when *you* have a good time.

9. But not enough to go with me.

10. No, not enough to go with you.

11. If you loved me, you'd go with me.

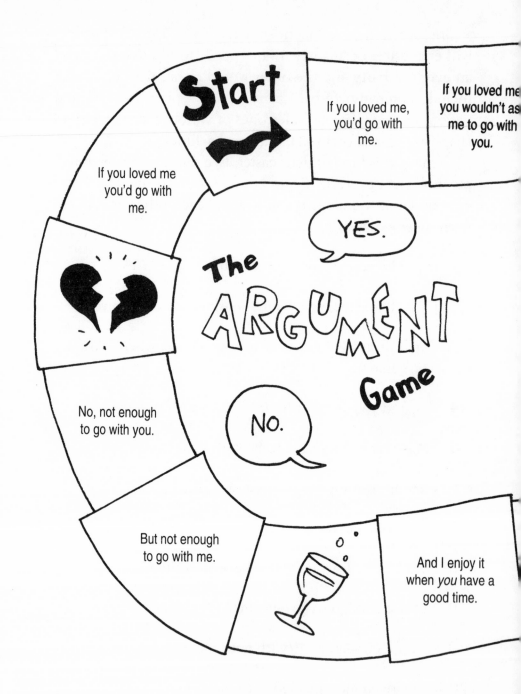

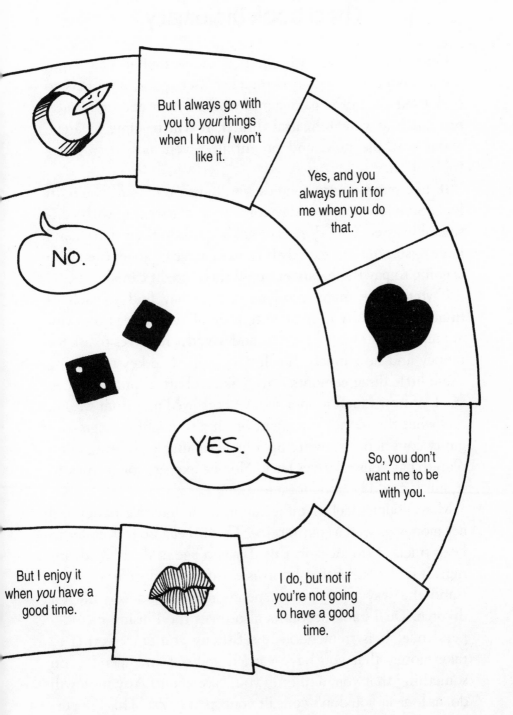

Checkbook Diplomacy

Once you've moved in together, and settled all your arguments about who gets how much closet space, who gets to park their car in the garage and whose best friend drank *way* too much at your rehearsal dinner, it will be time to argue about a whole new, and potentially even *more aggravating* topic: money.

If, like many young couples, you have no money, you're in luck. So many people today come to a relationship with considerable assets (i.e., dozens of credit cards in their name) and have to sort out just exactly how to manage finances (i.e., who is going to pay the balances on all those credit cards).

If you're like many newlyweds, you may find yourself in financial difficulty from time to time. This can lead to awful arguments over whose parents and wealthy relatives to ask for money and how much they'll cough up. The key to solving these little disagreements is to make a chart in order to keep track of how much money you've borrowed and from whom, and what the money was spent on. It also might assuage your guilty conscience to write up a little timetable charting out a plan to pay your relatives back. No one expects you to stick to it, but it could be good for a few laughs.

Many couples feel that it is important to have *his* money and *her* money as well as *our* money. This is because it is easier to keep track of finances in this day and age of dual breadwinners. It is also easier to split up assets after you decide you can't stand the way your spouse spends money and you file for divorce. Dual bank accounts also gives the illusion of independence. It is tremendously satisfying and empowering to take money that you have earned yourself and spend it on something that you, and only you, care about. Any item will do, as long as you don't consult your spouse first. This is a purchasing decision that you and you alone make. This is a great way to get over arguments and power struggles within the marriage. It will bring you much closer together as you each express your independence and your individuality. Also, when you sell off all the useless items you've bought for ten cents on the dollar, you'll realize that there's nothing like a garage sale to bring a couple together.

Of course, what veteran married couples know is that for a true thrill, there is nothing like shopping for something that you love and know your spouse will hate and buying it with your spouses's money. *That's* real empowerment.

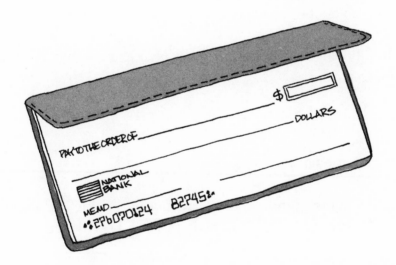

Terms of Endearment:
A List of Icky Nicknames

Once you fall in love and decide to tie the knot, it will no longer be OK simply to call your spouse "Francois" or "Corrine." Particularly if your spouse is not named "Francois" or "Corrine." Personally, I would have to punch anyone that had the nerve to call me Francois. What a sissy name. Corrine is kind of nice though. Anyhow, after you are married you will want to call each other by what therapists refer to as "Icky Nicknames." All couples do it. It indicates ownership.

After your first year is up you will begin to use your favorite "Icky Nicknames" during arguments with withering irony to bludgeon your spouse. Example: "So nice of you to leave the bathroom door open so we can all enjoy that wonderful smell, *honey.*"

To follow is a partial list of "Icky Nicknames" that you may want to try out.

1. Honeybunch

2. Sweetie Face

3. Pookums (and the derivatives, Pookie, Pookster, Pookarooski, The Pookmeister, Pook DeVille, etc.)

4. Snuggle Bunny

5. Loverboy

6. Baby Doll

7. Sugar Drawers

8. Mama or Daddy (as in "Who's my sweet Daddy?" and "Come to Mama.")

9. Pumpkin (or as people who use "Icky Nicknames" like to pronounce it "Punkin")

10. My Hunky Pair O' Giggledy Buns*

* Not in general use

These are acceptable for use in the first year of marriage but not thereafter, except as mentioned above.

Note: Baby talk in any form and at any time is unacceptable!

OOH, WHO'S MY WITTEW WOOGUMS? ARE YOU MY SWEETIE BOOTS? MY BABY CAKES? GEE, DON'T WE JUST WUV BEING MARRIED, HONEY BUNNY?

A Pre-Nuptial Agreement
You Can Really Use

Unless you're Donald Trump (and who would admit such a thing?), the standard pre-nuptial agreement is a thoroughly worthless piece of paper, which will only provide something for your lawyers to fight over when you divorce. Let's face it, if you were rich enough to need a pre-nuptial agreement you wouldn't be getting married.

Here, in standard legal form, is a pre-nuptial agreement that you can *really* use.

For Wives

1. I promise not to get fat like my sisters did right after they got married.

2. I promise not to talk to you the way my mother talks to my dad.

3. I promise to wear exciting underwear on occasion.

4. I promise not to talk about "freshness," feminine hygiene or yeast infections at the table.

5. I promise not to ask my husband about his *feelings* more than twice a year.

6. I promise not to tell my friends about what my husband does in bed.

7. I promise to limit my crying to sad movies and not to use it as a trump card during arguments.

8. I promise to limit the number of fuzzy and/or cute and adorable items I have to a number my husband can look at without throwing up.

9. I promise to let my husband have a "Boys Night Out" once in awhile and not ask him what he did 'til all hours of the morning.

10. I promise never to buy my husband slippers for Christmas.

Signed   _____

Date   _____

For Husbands

1. I promise not to get fat like my brothers did right after they got married.

2. I promise to limit my participation in male bonding sports (bowling, golf, softball, etc.) to twice weekly.

3. I promise to change diapers (wet and dirty) should the need arise.

4. I promise to talk about how I feel at least twice a year.

5. I promise to call.

6. I promise to come up with expensive jewelry at least every fifth anniversary and/or birthday.

7. I promise not to talk to my wife the way my dad talked to my mom.

8. I promise not to tell my friends what my wife wears to bed.

9. I promise to take my wife out on a "real date" at least once a month.

10. I promise never to give my wife a kitchen appliance for Christmas.

Signed   _____

Date   _____

Renewing Your Vows: For Wives

I, _____, take this man, and I use the term loosely, to be my lawfully wedded husband, even though my parents and friends think he's a major loser, to have, as if another woman would, and to hold, as long as he's had a shower recently, from this day forward.

For better—he better behave himself—and for worse—it better not get worse—in sickness, and in health, and when I'm having a P.M.S. day. For richer, like the day we got that new credit card, and for poorer, like the day he maxed it out by buying that new riding lawn mower.

To love, as much as I can love a man who constantly forgets to put the toilet seat back down and to honor, as much as I can honor a man who flirts with my sister every time he has three beers.

To love and to cherish, and to obey enough to let him think *he's* in charge, 'til death or attorneys do us part.

Renewing Your Vows: For Husbands

I, _____, take this woman to be my lawfully wedded wife, since I probably can't get out of this thing now, to have, as often as I want, and to hold just long enough, before we have sex, to call it foreplay, from this day forward.

For better—so she'll wear the teddy I bought her to bed at least *once* in awhile, and for worse—when she insists on wearing her favorite Mickey Mouse T-shirt instead. For richer, even though she won't understand why that bonus I got is going toward new golf clubs and not toward our "second honeymoon" vacation and for poorer, because I would've taken that promotion if it wouldn't have caused me to miss my softball league nights, and in sickness and in health, because hopefully she'll call in sick for me when I've got a tee time.

To love, and to cherish, as much as my new car, and to obey, enough to let her think *she's* in charge, 'til death, or attorneys, do us part.

Epilogue:
The Rabbit Did What?

Y ou are now truly a couple. You have worked out all your problems, small and big. He has learned to pick up your birth control pills at the drug store without blushing and you have learned just exactly how much milk he likes to have poured on his Fruit Loops® in the morning. He wouldn't think of buying orange juice with the pulp in it anymore and you always remember to slide the seat back where he likes it, after you drive his car. You also put the radio back on that stupid country station he listens to and put on the emergency brake, even though your driveway is perfectly flat, just because you know it drives him crazy if you don't.

You've reached a point in your marriage where your home is tranquil. Your rhythms complement each other. On your good days you are as in sync as the Boston Symphony Orchestra and on your bad days you at least still work together like a cheap watch.

You've reached a point where your arguments are free-spirited, evenly fought affairs which rarely necessitate a trip to the emergency room for stitches and X-rays. You never raise your voices or bring up hurtful subjects like cellulite or out of control nose hairs.

You've reached a point where you are both comfortable. You are happy and, darn it, you're still still in love with each other. You've reached a point ... where your home pregnancy test will come back positive.

Good luck.

This book is published by

PRICE STERN SLOAN
L o s   A n g e l e s

whose other hilarious humor books include:

The Everyday Guide to Everyday Stuff

A Guy Goes into a Bar

A Guy Goes to the Doctor

The Complete Murphy's Law

These and many other books may be bought wherever books are
sold or may be ordered directly from the publisher.

PRICE STERN SLOAN
L o s   A n g e l e s

11150 Olympic Boulevard, Sixth Floor
Los Angeles, CA 90064